J.P. Homer's

THE THESODDY

Written and illustrated by J. D. Peterson

Aventine Press

First Edition

Published by Aventine Press
1023 4th Ave #204
San Diego CA, 92101
www.aventinepress.com

ISBN: 1-59330-431-5

Printed in the United States of America

For my wife,
the love of my life,
and my children,
my own dar mofts.

INTRODUCTION TO J.P. HOMER

Far across the galaxy, or perhaps much, much closer, there is a tiny planet, named Orn, that has 17 moons. Few people on Earth know of this planet's existence, and even fewer believe that there is life there. However, years of careful research (by individuals who prefer to remain anonymous) have uncovered a rich body of literature from this planet. There are Ornian tales, full of heroes and villains, that may have had a significant influence on the myths and legends of our own tiny planet. Indeed, some have said that Ornians have visited Earth for thousands of years, exchanging tales with a few of our most famous early historians as well as with more contemporary writers.

The most well known of the Ornian writers, J.P. Homer, lived from 2148-2026 BE (Before Enlightenment, approximately Earth's 14,516 BC). Although human, J.P. Homer was orphaned at an early age and raised by a breed of silly, green, large-nosed humanoids known as dar mofts. This had a great effect upon his writings and profoundly shaped the philosophy with which he founded the *School of Lesser Historians* when he was just 12 years old. He named this school George, after the uncle he never had.

The titles of some of J.P. Homer's early works have been discovered, unfortunately without the stories, so we can only guess at the topics. These include **Of Dar Mofts and Men**, **The Guy Who Killed His Father and Married His Mother**, **The Ichthyad**, **The Three Guys (and Another One) with Swords**, **The Wizard of Orn**, **Frankenmoft** , **A Dinghy Named Desire**, **War and Peas**, and **Alice in Underwhere**, as well as dozens of others with themes or titles that often appear similar to later Earthly writings. Sadly, only a handful of Homer's stories have been discovered in complete form, usually lining old trunks, wrapped around fish, on the bottoms of bird cages, or buried in vaults of obscure museums.

Thus it was that, in the remnants of an abandoned house in Boston, Massachusetts, I discovered Homer's **The Thesoddy.** It had obviously been used to line several exotic bird cages, presenting some additional challenges in the translation of this material. (Unfortunately, the other challenge was that the pages weren't numbered). Written in 2048 BE, **The Thesoddy** is undoubtedly the oldest remaining intact Ornian history. It pre-dates both Alatar's **Bortlevin**, J.P. Homer's own **Homestead Trilogy**, and **The Siege of the Great Wall of D'Ung** (anonymous). Typical of many of J.P. Homer's histories, **The Thesoddy** portrays an epic hero of mostly normal proportions. This tale was apparently written as the history of the Gods' punishment of Freeny in 959 YOTG (Year Of The Gods, approximately 11,000 BE, give or take 10,000 years), chronicling the strange adventures of a minor noble who goes on a dangerous, absurd, and relatively short journey in the attempt to save his country.

Did this tale, written thousands of years before Earth's recorded history, influence our own Homer's *Odyssey*? I'll let you decide. At any rate, J.P. Homer's tales are shining examples of the Lesser Histories of Orn without which we would not have as many Lesser Histories of Orn.

J.D. Peterson

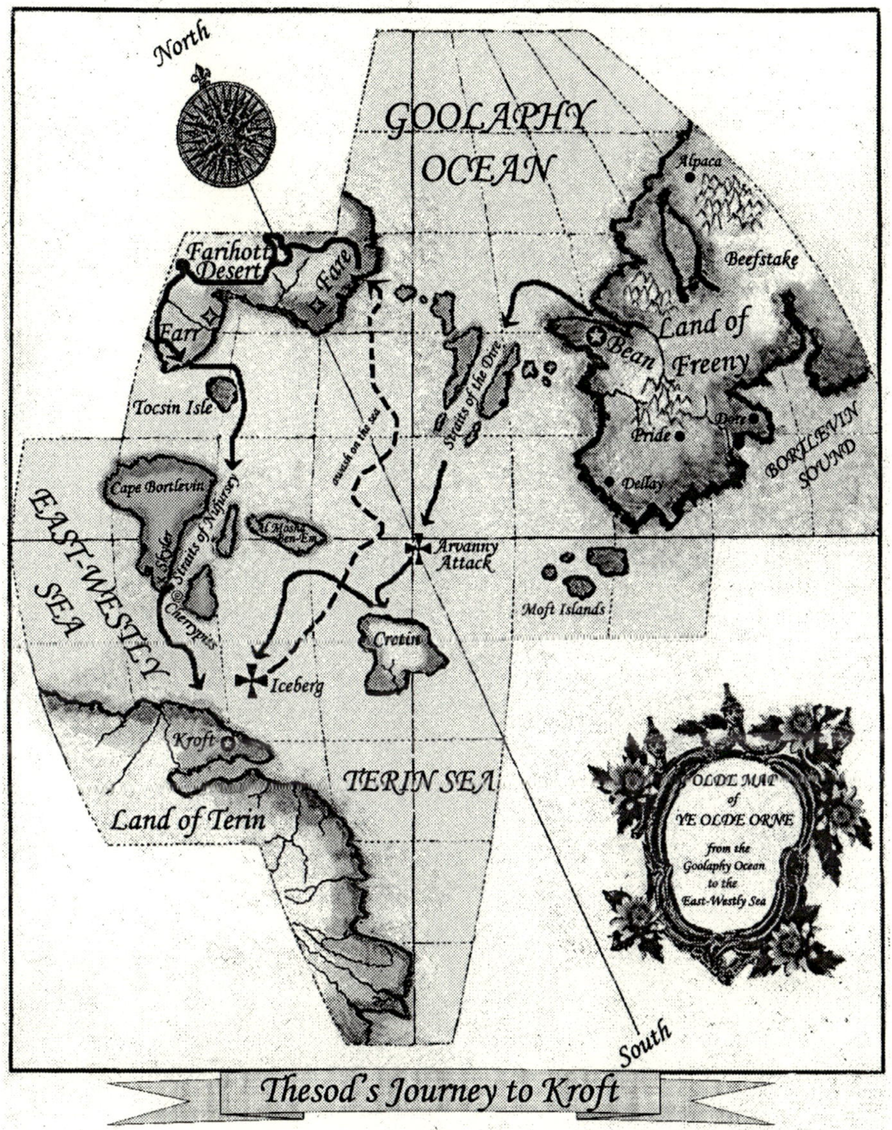
North
GOOLAPHY OCEAN
Alpaca
Beefstake
Land of Freeny
Bean
Pride
Dore
Dellay
BORLEVIN SOUND
Farihott Desert
Fare
Farr
Tocsin Isle
Straits of the Ore
awash on the sea
Cape Bortlevin
Straits of Nijursy
Skyler
Cherrypis
EAST-WESTEY SEA
Arvanny Attack
Moft Islands
Cretin
Iceberg
Kroft
Land of Terin
TERIN SEA
OLDE MAP of YE OLDE ORNE from the Goolaphy Ocean to the East-Westly Sea
South
Thesod's Journey to Kroft

TABLE OF CONTENTS

Part I. Insulting the Gods[1]

The Year of the Gods was just nine-fifty-nine,
and Freenian folk had much fun all the time.
Freeny was known for its culture and arts,
its very nice people, championship darts,
craggy white cliffs, and rough, rolling green hills,
the goodest cuisine and fine rubbersmith mills.

Freeny was pious, quite kind to the Gods,
and full of Godfellows who followed in mobs.
But, one stormy morn at the hour of When[2],
(the time for the offers to Moose[3] and his ken)
a dar moft[4] named Zed overslept in his shed,
forgetting the gift to the God of the Dead.[5]
Frabjously angered, this pasty-faced God
then sent down a beast, a large decapod,
to frighten and bully the Freenian folk
with roars, and blue slime, and a face like egg yolk.

Zed is Late

Soon Moose and the rest of the Gods in Olmpoo[6]
sent down their plagues to punish them too.
There were rains and large fires (although not the same time),
and Banshoos, and Reeboks, and Great Killer Mimes[7].
Monsters that raged at the end of long days
were replaced by night beasties with red eyes ablaze.
Bean, that fair city of Freenian fame,
was stalked by Red Languids[8] and Horricious Sames[9].

Freenfolk were fearful and crouched behind doors
of tiny Freenhovels[10] to hide from the gore,
while out in the streets and the lanes of Bean town
the beasties grabbed stone walls and tore them all down.
Unlucky Freenians, caught unaware,
were most promptly eaten, all boots, clothes, and hair.
Fires consumed and charred many a home,
leaving no mark but a square of black loam
where before was an otherwise beautiful place.
The Gods did make Bean a God-awful disgrace.
Even the farmlands of country of Freen
saw beasties and plagues which they never had seen
in all their long lives (or their grandfathers' too).
There wasn't a thing that these farmfolk could do

Assault on Freeny

as Great Killer Mimes very silent destroyed
their crops and their burden-beasts, all of their joy.

Many days passed as the people did hide
all locked away safe, with families inside.
Was there no answer to this awful fate?
Did they just have to sit quiet and wait
'til nothing was left of the land that they knew?
Or . . . was there a Hero come out of the blue
with shimmering sword and an attitude keen
to challenge the beasties and regain their Freen?

With yelling and cheers, from out of a door,
Mighty Young Joe[11] stepped outside to the war.
Bean-folk peered out at this ape of a man.
"If Joe cannot do it, then nobody can!"
He raised mighty fists to the beasties about,
daring attack and inviting them out
to be pummeled and beaten and feel his sharp knife.
A large Grat[12] stepped on him and snuffed out his life.

Bean's royal advisors strained baldly-domed heads.
How could they placate the God of the Dead?
The King was depressed and the Queen was afraid,
yet brained and outrageous a good plan was laid.
What Freeny did need was some help from a God,
(a God who was not too averse to hob-knob
with mortals), a God who could tell all the rest
that ending this punishment really was best.

In troubles and strife good King Idle of Bean
could think of no other but Thesod, the Freen,
so Idle of Freeny sent Thesod to Kroft[13]
with a kree[14] made of lead and a crew of dar mofts.
The goal, it was blessings from Goddess above:
Great Afrodainty's[15] sweet powers of Love.

Part II. Thesod of Freeny

Thesod of Freeny was handsome and brave
with more strength than Bernaffy[16], more wits than Elaive[17],
a good-natured demeanor that all folk admired,
and a fondness for wearing quite snappy attire.
And Thesod of Freeny had finer points, too!
There were very few things that this man couldn't do.
He was Prince of Alpaca[18], the Duke of Beefstake[19],
and a sailor of prowess (he oft sailed on a lake).

His finest of talents was stupendous luck,
the finding of means when the ways were amuck.
For who but this man could survive a bad fall
from out of his window and over the wall,
missing the moat by a full fifty fleet[20],
and landing in passing cartwheels of wheat.
"A fluke!" one might say, "or just planned to amaze!"
The fact still remains that he wasn't fazed.

Again and again this had happened to him,
the salt-flats of Vermin, the Grand Cliffs of Tim,

And many more others alike in one way:
Thesod of Freeny survived them some way.

Heroes are favored by Hairless, the Blue[21],
the Goddess of Guts (and of Imbeciles, too).
She rarely helped Thesod, since he had such luck,
but did lend her hand if brave Thesod was stuck
between a hard place and a very large rock,
with no chance of safety and nowhere to walk.
But Hairless would wait up until the last Last[22]
before helping anyone out of some nast,[23]
bad fate at the hands of some bullicious[24] foe.
She wanted some guts and some braveness to show.
Often enough, Hairless waited too late
leaving a hero to some messy fate
in the jaws of some beastie with pewnut[25]-sized mind.
She saw plenty of guts . . . but not the right kind.

Without ever asking, she once sent Thesod
to slay some small dragnets in Baldwort on Skrod[26]
that were tormenting good folks inside of their homes
with nibbles and bitings and breakings of bones.
Oddly enough, the mad dragnets were small

and really could hardly be seen, if at all.
A full-grown dragnet was but 50 rongs[27] size,
(the size of the thumbnails of quite big-thumbed guys).
A herd of these dragnets, these nastly, nast beasts,
could bring down a fully-grown Grat, at the least.

When Thesod arrived at plagued Baldwort's Skrod Bay
he pondered their plight and considered a way
to lure dragnets out and attack them by sword
(really small swords made of tin-spines from cord[28]).
The beasties came out when he whistled the call[29]
that love-lonely she-beasts use late in the fall.
Dragnets swarmed over poor Thesod and swords,
not even hurt by Thesod's spinal cord.

Then Thesod yelled mighty, from deep in his lungs,
a word that was so thunderous that it stung
the hides of the dragnets and made them fall dead
at the feet of mad Thesod, like so much dry bread.
To win in defeat in so strange of a way
did baffle brave Thesod 'til end of his days,
but, nevertheless, he stomped 'round the town
yelling quite loudly to bring dragnets down.

Thesod, e'er-after, was drafted for more,
the Goo-cats of Balsa[30], the Velcros of Dore[31],
the wimps of Dellay[32], and the twiggies of Pride[33].
With luck Thesod barely did scratch his fair hide.
His mission to Kroft was a dangerous chore,
fraught full of beasties, perhaps much, much more.
Objections from Thesod? Nay, nary a peep,
for Thesod, poor Thesod, was still fast asleep.
When crow called the morning, its beak to the sun,
his castle, his moat, and his town he saw none.

Thesod and the Dar Mofts

Part III. Not much help from Hairless

The kree was three-masted, named Lady Of Brine,
with sleek hull of lead and the sails weaved of tine[34],
and she sloshed along weighty, waves parting like dreck,
as Thesod, grave Thesod, strode onto the deck.
Dar mofts grinned onely, green schnozzes a-laugh,
with mirthing and dancing, much lint to belaff[35].
They eyed their brave Captain, their straight-man . . . Oh, good,
awake for some ribbing . . . as much as they could.

Dar mofts are green, and have pointy green heads,
garnished but slightly with small tufts of red
on their points, and on wrists, and on wide ankles, too.
Large toothy smiles they will use right on cue.
A dar moft makes jokes at the drop of a hat
(or the drop of most any such object as that).
They live for the silly; they don't do much work.
They chuckle and whistle and act like green jerks . . . .
This is in front of their masters, at least.
In private they talk of the teachings of Neeste[36],

Philosophy, Physics, Kantusian Plains[37],
the Theories of Gauche[38], or the healing of pains.
Debates get quite heated, their voices get raised . . . .
but when Master enters they start acting dazed.
They gyre[39] and they daper[40] and belaff their lint
'til master retires . . . not even a hint.

One can't blame Thesod for looking quite grave
with crew not full-brained and a country to save.
"Save me Blue Hairless, the Goddess of Guts.
I have a great mission. My crew is quite nuts.
Grant me a crew trained in sailing and lore.
Grant me this, please!" did Thesod implore.
"Are you a baby?" she asked of the man.
"Frightened of trying when ship hits the sand!
Be a big boy, not a wailing young tot.
Maybe I'll help you . . . maybe I'll not."
His pleanings[41] unanswered, he firmed his resolve.
"This mission I'll finish. This problem I'll solve."

So Thesod worked hardly to train the dar mofts
for toiling at wheel or in rigglings[42] aloft.
But dar mofts could not figure out all their chores,

Hairless, Goddess of Guts

falling asleep and then snorting loud snores.
Often a dar moft threw something away,
discarding an anchor, or jar of kree's clay[43],
the sail-weaving tine, or the night's dinner swill,
angering Thesod so much he could kill.

"Shape up, moft-swabbies!" did mad Thesod cry.
"Learn all you chores, or we might just all die
in the mouth of some scum-sucking beastie at sea.
Learn all you chores or that's what our fate be."
He drilled them through drills and contingency plans,
plotting out footsteps of each every man.
He planned everything to the minnest [44]detail,
but each every time all the dar mofts did fail.

They tripped on their feet and they stood in the way
of Thesod as he tried to do what he may
to finish the drill or at least part of it.
He flung up his hands and said, "Dar mofts are twits."

So, then Thesod tried a bit different track,
telling the dar mofts to try to stand back.
This they could do with no straining at all,

quite gracefully dodging[45] all work that did fall
within one arm's reach or a footstep or four.
They quickly, completely avoided all chores.
Both Thesod and dar mofts were happy this way.
Thesod toiled hard, and the dar mofts did lay
on the sidelines just watching their brave captain work,
while whustling[46], belaffing and acting like jerks.
They prided themselves that they helped out their kree
by being themselves and just letting things be.

Part IV. The quiet and the storming

The sea spread out like a wide desert of foam,
green-blue topped with whitecaps, a wet land to roam.
Dar mofts lay out in their deck-chairs all oiled
and soaking up rays of the sun 'til they broiled,
and they hooted with laughter like drunk dipsobirds[47],
while Thesod swabbed deck-boards and glared at these nerds.
Then dar mofts grabbed mops, and they danced 'round the deck,
all joking with Thesod and giving him heck.
His eyes became angry, his face became gruff . . .
showing his crew that he had had enough . . . .
but then Thesod laughed, and he smiled at his crew.

He said, "By the Gods! I'll dance with you, too.
It's too fair a day for such working as this.
I'll cease my deck-swabbing and join in your bliss."
The crew gaped in wonder. Old Stoneface unwind?
He was a kind man . . . though who knew **what** kind.
They had a small feast and played young dar moft games[48].
They did all this once, and they then did the same.
When playtime was over, the captain and crew
returned[49] to do work with their thoughts freshed anew.

Three days did unwind as they sailed on to Kroft,
then white clouds turned darker and roiled all aloft.
The dar mofts and Thesod sensed weather aboil,
and mofts started dancing while Thesod did toil
to maintain the ship between tall, wavy heads
and not bucking wildly, this kree made of lead.

On choppy waves bouncing, through spasms of stone[50],
past sandbars and coral in dread shallow zones,
Thesod was guided by Hairless the Grand
to stay in the waters and off of the land.
He missed the sharp rocks sticking out from the right,
spinning kree's wheel 'til it nearly took flight.
He swerved hard again to miss rocks on the left,
with arms muscle-strong and his fingers quite deft
at moving red knobs and blue levers apace[51].
The stake was their lives in this sea-stormy race.

Soon came the time to abandon the wheel
to the kree's autopilot [52]as Lady did reel
from buffeting rains on her sails weaved of tine.
Thesod climbed mast to save Lady Of Brine.

He uncurled the sails to their widest extent
to outrun the storming, so deadly intent
to sink the fine kree as she sailed toward Kroft.
Then all at once, Thesod fell from aloft!
If not for the line which was looped 'round his feet,
Thesod and kree would have surely been beat.
But Hairless had guided brave Thesod's fine fate,
and when he fell down she made sure he weren't late[53].
The rope 'round his feet stopped him inches from death,
sparing his life but near stealing his breath.
Downside-up dangling he unsheathed his sword,
losing no time in quick-cutting the cord.
He rolled to his feet, dodging dar mofts to right,
and retook the wheel as the Lady took flight
from the storm and the winds that filled her great sails.
They sailed in front of the worsening gale.

Blackened clouds grumbled . . . the bellies shot fire,
as Lady Of Brine fled through Straits of the Dire[54].
Lightning struck nearly, the thunder whammed loud,
yet Lady fled onward with sails held up proud.
Waves strained her sidings, wind battered her sail.
Black rocks were ahead! The Lady might fail!

The dar mofts moved into the decks down below,
loud-miming[55] and singing and having a show,
while Thesod hauled mighty at wheel and at sheet,
. . . bringing the Lady around. What a feat!
Rocks were avoided and waters 'came still.
All became well . . . quite well . . . until . . . ,
Geeroffaneefy, the God of the Sea,
sent an arvanny[56] to sink Thesod's kree.

The Storming

Part V. The sea beastie

Seven heads jawing and snapping sea-foam
suggested to Thesod he wasn't alone.
Horrendicous shrieks and brine-splashing green tails,
it had smelly, foul breath, and skin-scales like chain mail.
The arvanny stalked the fine Lady Of Brine,
winding its way, and slow-taking its time,
sizing its prey in its greeny-eyed way,
with much oofing and orting[57] in pleasure of play.
A feint to the left, and a feint to the straight,
a nip at the Lady, then beastie would wait.
For hours it played with the crew and her kree
like naughty narkitty[58] with rat up a tree.

Arvanny did not fear its prey in the least.
This was its home . . . and this was its feast.
It relished the fear in the eyes of its meals . . .
but saw no such thing in the man at the wheel.
The man stared back brandly[59], no yellowness there.
The courage that showed was exceedingly rare.

The Arvanny

Thesod walked toward the arvanny's hide
with left hand on sword and his right by his side.
He fancied with blade, the tip whizzing so quick
that it blurred in one's sight and made one feel sick
as he slashed at the air . . . a right deadly sight,
a display of blade-prowess and great swordly might[60].

He looked at arvanny, expecting to see
the seeds of blade-fear in this beastie at sea.
Sea-beastie laughed, a stench-rotty exhale,
at the sight of this hero, all hardy and hale,
who thought he could scrap with a beast of its frame.
Apparently Thesod did not know this game.

Beastie dived deep to the innards of sea,
a-gathering speed 'til it turned on a T.
Returning speedquick to the kree up above,
it smatt Lady's hull with a hugendous shove.
The kree remained wholesome but flew from the waves,
scores high in the air, a beast-toy enslaved
to the will of a beastie which waited below
with tails poised for smatting another dread blow.

Thesod leaned over the rail of the kree
as she fell back to water to see what he'd see.
He called to arvanny, "What's that over there?"
and pointed to sunward and into the glare.
Arvanny, distracted, gazed into the sun
as Lady fell on it, all fifty Freen-tons[61].
Though beast wasn't hurt much, just lumped on the heads,
it was muchly angered and plainly saw red.

Thesod held sword high and maintained his wits
as sea-beast approached in a seaspastic fit[62].
He sparred with beast heads and beast tails from all 'round
with slash to the fore and then back with a bound,
doing no damage but staying unharmed
as slimed teeth did snap at his face and sword-arm.
Sword glanced off scales just as hard as pig-tin,
blunting the blade and not letting it in.
Then brave Thesod tripped over ropes on the deck,
flying forefirst to the rail hard as heck,
and his sword flew out straight to a small, scaleless spot,
puncturing deep the large beast that he fought.

The arvanny bellowed its fighting-pain cry[63]
and raised up its heads with it's rearing[64] up high.
One head veered left, and the other six straight,
(straight at our Thesod, thus sealing his fate).

Yet, Zed the Dar Moft held a bottle in hand,
of Beastie Remover[65] (the Triple-strength Brand).
Three teency drops on the scales of one head
were all that was needed to make it fall dead.
It sagged and it whuffled, expelling foul breath
on the dar mofts and Thesod, and sank to its death.
Thesod set sail for the far shores of Kroft
with dead sea-beastie odors a-swirling aloft.

Part VI. Land of the goo-berry eaters

The wisers[66] foretold of the coming of he
who would brave the nast forces[67] at work in the sea.
Would Gods be his downfall? Would mission be done?
Would Great Afrodainty renew Freeny's fun?
Thesod knew not if the mission'd be won,
but by God and by folly he'd sail to the sun.
If that's what was needed to save his fine ken,
he'd sail there and back by the hour of Then[68].

They sailed for three months, through storm and through still,
'til starving of thirst and a bit low on swill,
Thesod found land and a town for his crew
to gather supplies and to sluck[69] down some brews,
(or take in some movies, an opera or two),
and sleep in wide beds that were stuffed with soft thew[70].

The Hotel Calypso[71] was run by Miss Muse.
The rooms were quite large . . . filled with all one could use.
Goo-berries plenty they dined on by hands
of pretty, young girl-serfs from wayafar lands.
All of their wantings were filled to the max,

even fine whine[72] or a spine-jazzing sax.
While Thesod was dazed by this living so soft,
dar mofts danced femly fem, comely yar mofts[73]
who looked at them lovely with big, bulgous glims[74],
and top-knots to die for, these yar mofts so slim.

Each every day was a blessing to them,
with new friendly friends and attentions of fems.
Miss Muse insisted that all things were free
and fattened them up with broiled fezzik and ghee[75],
red-hot vats of sheckin[76], cold tankards of ade,
persemmins of cake[77], and sweet biscuits sooflayed.
Legions of porters would not let them walk,
and carried them all in fine chairs gilt with mock[78].

Day after day, fine massages received,
their muscles were softened and limbs were relieved.
by laying in steambaths, all dressed in gilt towels,
'til unable to move or to utter a vowel.
Then porters removed them to rest in the shade
and plied them with more sweets and tankards of ade.

Drunken and blissed the kree's crew lay and gazed
while girl-serfs and yar mofts danced languid and lazed,
all dressed in fine woolies and scarves of slick nyle.
The brave crew was captive to feminine smiles.
Each every day brought surprises anew,
fattening them up and befuddling them, too.
When 10 days had passed and they knew they must go,
the crew and our hero did not want to know.
Lulled by soft living, enchanted by Muse,
all offers to stay there they could not refuse.

Muse brought goo-berries and poppy-gum squid[79],
grew glaze on their eyeballs . . . drooping their lids,
and took them downstairs all en-bundled in rags
to dungeon of Eelba, the Goddess of Hags[80].

The dar mofts and Thesod slept sound in the dark,
their lives foreverly losing their sparks.
Yet Vim had remained on the deck of their kree,
watching the island and minding the sea.
When Thesod and dar mofts were late by days five,
Vim went to find whether they be alive.

Land of the Goo-berry Eaters

Vim crept around softly, on whispering toes,
through woods and to town to determine if foes
had snared our snide hero or taken his brain[81],
quill-tickled his footsies, or given him pain.
Asudden he heard Mistress Muse and her hags
a-laughing their laughs and a-wagging their wags[82].
They laughed about Thesod and all his green goons.
Muse told 'tween great bouts of laughter that soon
White Eelba[83] would come to their dank cell below
to turn their wrapped bodies to Goo-berry dough,
for the making of bread from which Goo-berries rise,
for lulling of sailors . . . creating of pies.

Part VII. Thing for the Goddess

Vim dressed himself in black haggish long cowl
and looksied to see where to find dungeon foul.
A dark doorway hid by a skraggly fur tree[84]
looked likely to lead to where dungeon would be.
The stairway led down to the Goo-berry room,
chock-full of gooed sailors in Goo-berry doom.
Great spinners[85] blocked all the doorways with spores
and stick-sticky webbing . . . but not dungeon's door.
Vim sneaked to dungeon and poor Thesod's cell
to pluck at the lock there that locked them in hell.

Along came Great Eelba, a Goddess enraged
that her sluicy[86] captives might spring from their cage,
so Vim lobbed a cauldron to cover her face,
resuming pick-locking at frumious[87] pace.
One eye on the Goddess and one on his work,
he opened the cage with a terrific jerk.
He wakened brave Thesod by tickling his toes
and wakened each dar moft by tweaking his nose,
when all of a sudden a whiny yell rose,
with Eelba, Hag Goddess, in horrible pose.

She bolstered herself to let loose her mad power[88],
expecting her prey to just fall down and cower,
but weren't she surprised when what she did find
were dar mofts and Thesod admiring some kind
of rock or some rubbish all slimy and black,
ignoring Great Eelba's horrendous attack.
It must be right worthful for them to ignore
a Goddess all rattled and ready for gore.
Intrigued and quite puzzled and turning insane,
the Goddess approached them on hobbling cane.

"What is that you have there?" she asked hatefully.
"Is it pretty and worthful and worthy of me?
A bauble, perhaps, or a diamond engrimed.
What is that you have there? Stop wasting my time."
Thesod rose stiffly with careful reply,
"It's not worth your trouble. To you I won't lie.

This Thing[89] may be magic, but just for vain stuff.
To Goddess like you that would not be enough."
"Give it to me," she said to the man.
"I'll take it right now. Believe me I can."

Thesod said slowly, "It's not worth a ding[90]
if you don't know the right way to chant to the Thing."

"I'll make a bargain on Hatees[91] below.
We'll give you this prize if you let us all go.
In payment I'll tell you the chant you must sing
that may give you great beauty (or truth of this Thing).
You must say it just like I say it to you,
or I won't be at fault and the blame be yours, too.
Whatever may happen, we all must be freed.
Take it or leave it. This Thing's all we need."
"What must I say? Please tell me," she cried.
"Please do not take Thing away from my side."
"Then say this fast thrice to reveal its true force,"
said Thesod quite bravely, "correctly, or course.

Say 'Weering-bik tropple. Darmoft-zwee bestwokk.
Ziss thinggiz nothangbut tallarge dir Teerock[92].'"
So Eelba tried thrice, just as fast as she could,
but missed all three times, though her effort was good.
She bade them to go as she cradled her Thing,
chanting and trying correctly to sing

Eelba, Goddess of Hags

to a chunk of black rubbish, all slimy and black.
She had greed in her eyes with her mind on one track.
So Thesod and dar mofts escaped from their hell,
using muck from the floor and a rock from the cell.

In the distance they heard a great, ringing yell-scream.
Daft Eelba discovered the truth of mad dreams[93].
With compass consulted and the food stored below,
the captain and crew were all readied to go,
so Thesod of Freeny continued to Kroft,
with his kree made of lead and his crew of dar mofts.

Part VIII. The shipwrecking

Life came real easy in mid of the sea.
East winds were cool and the food was all free.
Dar mofts fished fish from the choppy green waves
with bivalve-hair line[94] and long curled bamboo staves.
With jibbie eggs spined over hook on the line
they lured deep sea fishies to make dining fine.

These months on the sea, there were but minor beasts
which didn't slow down Thesod's kree in the least.
Plattoods[95] hurled triteness and boring remarks
and swimmed round the hull of the kree in the dark,
while pantomymes[96] gestured in sad, lonely ways
in the mid of the sea in the brightness of day.
Wet deepsea snufflers[97] and wave-skimming squid,
fanged spirowets[98] and a heron named Sid,
were annoying, unnerving, and sometimes quite rude,
but they weren't all that bad (and they sometimes were food).

Thesod oft studied the stars and the moons
to guide him to Kroft with his band of green goons,
but sometimes the clouds overtook the blue sky,

forcing the captain on brains to rely.
He'd read the sea cues, probe the sky's cloudy lid,
and reason out where starry forms[99] should be hid
to plot out the way that his fine kree should head.
But, reasoning kree's course in this way he did dread,
for mid-sea hid dangers at this time of year,
keeping most sailors at home out of fear.
And commonly krees could be blown miles off track,
since winds could asudden unleash an attack.

After three months on the wave-choppy sea,
the winds whickered down to but whisper the kree.
Oceans were calmed, skies were clearer than glass,
and land on horizon was plush with tall grass.
Winds did quite gently blow breeze at the tines,
coaxing and soothing the Lady Of Brine
as lands scrolled by slowly and Kroft became near
to the eyes of brave Thesod through scope as he peered.
His eyes could see castles with spires high above
and temples of Great Afrodainty of Love.

Thesod's heart smelled[100] with the pride of this day.
He and his crew had traversed the whole way

to Kroft. They'd finished their long, risky cruise,
sure that the Goddess would never refuse
his plea for his kinfolk back home in fair Freen.
(By now back in Freeny the times must be lean.)

Great Afrodainty was known for her heart.
She never refused a brave man any part
of her talents to make his life better awhile.
She helped all brave men, with a wind-breaking smile.
To Thesod perhaps she'd grant favors entire,
pleasing his wishes and curing the dire.
Thesod's thoughts blanned[101] as he gazed at the land
and pondered the future of him and his band.

All was at peace as the kree left deep sea
to enter the waters round Kroft, calm and free.

Then, out of a dustwind Quickslivver[102] appeared
with message for Thesod and news much afeared
that Moose and the rest of the Gods in Olmpoo
decided that Thesod's long mission weren't through.
Quickslivver bowed, and he clicked his quick heels,
saying, "Sorry, good man, I know how you feel.

But you'll get there soon . . . just not right away.
. . . and look out for that iceberg ahead, by the way!"
The warning was late for the kree to be saved.
The Lady Of Brine sank down under the waves.

Had Thesod called Hairless to fly him aloft,
he really could easy have made it to Kroft.
But as brave, goodfull captain, he pondered his crew
and stayed on the Lady until she was through.
Dar mofts float well but our Thesod did not.
In brackish green waters the captain was caught.

Quickslivver, Messenger of the Gods

Part IX. The Fare maiden

Covered with seaweed and face-down in sand,
Thesod awoke on the beach of some land
with reddish-green planties and lots of blue rocks,
as well as land crabbies[103] that pulled at his socks.
He was dreadfully weakish, and only could crawl
to the blue rocks beside him stacked up in a wall.
He pulled himself upright and peeked over it
and out of embarrassment near had a fit,
for yonder the wall flumed a small bathing jet[104]
and a comely young princess unclothed and all wet.
Our hero had braved many beasties and foes,
but could not withstand a cute girl with no clothes.
And so with a groan, he passed out complete
from exhaustion, embarrassment, and the sun's heat.

Sunlight streamed in through stone windows of blue
as Thesod awoke to the morning crow's cue.
Framed in the sunshine, her hair all a-fanned,
the beach princess sat near him, holding his hand
in her delicate hands, smooth, soft, and cool,
and asked how he came to have swooned by her pool.

"I cannot remember a thing before now,
about when I came here or not even how.
I cannot dredge up from my brain, stiff and sore,
my name or my country or anything more."
This Thesod said with a tear in his eye
but thanked her for nicely not letting him die.

The maiden blushed rosely and shyly replied,
"I think you're acute, and I'm glad you came by.
I welcome you well to the fair land of Fare[105].
Drink of our water and breathe in our air
and soon you'll be weller than ever you've been,
(should you remember your wheres and your whens).
Sleep you some sleep and perhaps dream some dreams
so your head can 'come well . . . not apart at the seams."

The maiden, named Syrinx[106], showed Thesod all Fare
and all of the folkies who had settled there,
as well as the castles and ritzy, fine grounds
with their snubby-rich nobles and snooty hunt-hounds.
Thesod and Syrinx spent much time in fun,
enjoying their time from day-start to day-done

picnicking, laughing, and basking in shade,
and swimming green waters with bottoms of jade.

Soon Thesod realized that he was in love
with pretty-eyed Syrinx, his featherless dove.
He no longer tried to remember his name,
or country, or purpose, or how he had came
to the country of Fare and this land far astray
from the rest of the world (which was far, far away).

Strangely askance[107] he kept seeing green men
with pointy green heads with red tufts on them.
They followed Thesod and his maidenly friend,
acting real quiet, quite quiet, and then . . .
just when they passed by forgetfull Thesod
they looked somewhere else (or maybe they'd nod)
but they whispered something from the side of their lips,
"Your name is Thesod, you silly old dip!"

At night when our Thesod dream-sleeped in his bed,
he oft heard soft chanting from far above-head
and dreamed he saw greenish men dangling on vines

outside his window reciting this line:
"Thesod O'Thesod our brave captain true
come to us now, we're your slaphappy crew."

For twenty-two nights and the same count in days
blank Thesod heard whispers and chants, and adaze . . .
he suddenly realized "I'm Thesod by Gods,
and I've got a mission. I have a job!"
He left lovely Syrinx, but promised to come
to her once again when his mission was done.
Thesod was saddened, and Syrinx was grave,
but he left with his dar mofts, his Freeny to save.

Thesod and Syrinx

Part X. Never eat a camel

With no kree to sail and no sense in the least,
sad Thesod and band could but only stomp east,
across a nast desert all sandy and dry,
and full of dread nomads unfearful to die.
Bones of dead beasties and forsaken sods
littered the sand underfoots that they trod.
No trees or shrubbies sprang up from the ground,
just meat-eating cacti[108] all vicious and brown,
while under each rock that they passed, critters dwelt
who scuttled or slithered or dreadnastful smelt[109].

The sun's heat fried down on eight green, pointy brains
(and one rounded one) as they prayed hard for rain.
Only camel stayed cool, but his temper was hot.
(He spurned to bear loads of the goods that they brought.)
So, fully enloaded with swill and supplies
Thesod and dar mofts felt like Sherpa guys[110],
as camel danced 'round them in horrible sun,
while kicking them hard and then spitting for fun.
(Camel spit isn't the most pleasing kind
of thing to have drying up on your behind).

After two weeks in the desert so harsh
they came across footprints of many amarch,
including a camel, who seemed to be-dance
about nine tired men. More victims of chance?
They hadn't seen anyone else on their trek.
Where could they be, these unknown rejects?
Then Thesod realized the problem they had.
They had fully circled. This was real bad.
Syrinx had given them swill and supplied
enough to sustain them to farway Farr[111] side.
But she hadn't foreseen that they might crave a guide,
like a map or a compass to save all their hides.
Needless to say, they all wandered a lot
'til they ran out of swill and the water they brought.

After five days full of hunger and thirst,
they eyed their nast camel and pondered the worst.
The dar moft named Vim built a fire quite high
with dry husks of sagebrush and brownied cacti.
Zed sharpened a spit (just about camel size),
then the camel, though dumb, did begin to realize
the extent of his danger among these green louts.
He rolled up his eyes, and he then passed right out.

With camel a-spit and a fire aflame,
our Thesod and crew did not feel quite the same
as they had for five days. They felt better in fact
(now that they licked what for five days they lacked).
They feasted on roast hump and fried camel lips,
with soup dromedare and broiled camel hide strips.
They had camel meat sandwiches left for the long,
long trip they still had. It would help them stay strong.

Nomads had glared at them over the dunes
as they'd eaten the camel and sung eating tunes.
These nomads followed a God named Nonhorse[112],
the God of humped beasties (yes, camels of course).

This God did forbid any hump-munching types
and drafted cruel laws for these ones to be wiped
from the face of the desert. There was no excluse[113].
Nonhorse's laws were full-backed by High Moose.

So nomads weren't pleased by the feasting they saw
and vowed full revenge at the hands of their law.
They quick-ran downslope from their campsite up high
on the dunes as they screamed out their nomad deathcry[114].

Their swords all flashed bright as they cut through the wind
and ragely surrounded the ones who had sinned.

Brave Thesod raised up and brandished his sword
and firm held his footing against the mad horde,
but he tripped on the skull of a long-dead phantize[115],
unearthing a Book[116] that seemed ancient and wise.
His sword flew away as he fell to the sand,
surrounded by nomads and feeling un- grand.

Lifesaver

Part XI. Nomad Hatter

The nomads gazed down at sprawled Thesod in awe,
amazed at the man and the sight that they saw.
The Book by his feets was a tome from their past,
a listing of "happenwoulds", things that will pass.
The cover showed Thesod's thin, grizzly face,
and named him LIFESAVER, a comer from grace.

Was Thesod their king? Was he destined to be
the one who would lead them to life that was free
of their nast, sandy fate in this dry, dusty land.
Or was this a joke . . . just look at this man.
His clothes were rip-shabby. His skin was sunburned.
This new reputation was hardly well earned.
Could Thesod hunt down blue sand-guppies[117] by night
without any sawblade or even torchlight?
Could he locate the water that hid down below
'tween layers of hemrock[118] and plaks of sand-joe[119]?
None thought he could (nor did Thesod, of course),
but this Book was authored by Great God Nonhorse.
No choice in the least, they made Thesod King
of the Nomads by Farr and their land . . . everything.

Thesod considered the choices at hand,
thinking his only way out of this land
was to play-act at kingness and take charge today.
These nomads were brutish and likely to fray
if they doubted his right to this dry, sandy throne.
With just one mistake he'd be pushing up bones.

The dar mofts weren't bothered by this desert threat
and greeted each nomad like old friend well met.
Vim, Zed, and Gom whistled tunely moft-pipes[120],
getting the nomads to jig-dance en-hyped.
Scuffing up sand with their rapidfull toes,
their play-shrieks aloudly to heavenward rose,
while rest of the nomads came down from their camp
to bring Thesod finelies to wear and aclamp.
The women were scornfull of Thesod the King
but humbled reluctantly to the whole thing.
They oft-times knew better than nomadly spice[121]
but held their tongues quiet . . . 'til knowing the price.

The nomad named Hatter, the ex-boss of all
the nomads, was frabjously angered. The gall!
That a shabby wimp-stranger should take up his job

at very slight mention by Nonhorse the God!
So, while Thesod gave orders that all should stomp east
to border of Farr at the minimal least,
(and perhaps on to Kroft with this large, desert band),
Hatter the nomad had planned different plans.
He sneaked to the south to the ruins of Morse[122]
to look for more Books that were writ by Nonhorse[123].
[*His roadmap to Morse was all scribbled in code*
of dashes and dottings, and it did not bode
very well for old Hatter (who could not read Morse),
so he crumpled it up and he tossed it, of course.]
He prayed for the blessing of Nonhorse, the Humped,
to find ruined Morse and the Books that were dumped.

Half a day later, at quarter to Where[124],
nomad Hatter found Morse and discovered that there
were quite many editions of Nonhorse's Book.
He sauntered around there and had him a look.

The Book with Thesod on the cover (the gnome!)
was the first of editions of this holey tome.
The second edition was sorely revised,
and it offered excuses for being unwise

at naming brave Thesod the SAVER OF LIVES.

(Mistakes in translation had caused all this jive).

The true designation of Thesod, the Freen,

was EATER OF CAMELS WITH UGLY FRIENDS GREEN.

"Callooh and Callay![125]" shouted Hatter, well pleased.

"We'll carve up that Thesod. Gods **will** be appeased."

He sprinted east-north to his nomadly kind

to let them all know of the real truth this time.

Nomad Hatter

Part XII. Defense of offense: Camel slander

Nomads were told by mad Hatter, their boss,
of the big, big mistake they had made. Nothing lost!
For nomads rejoiced at the thought of redress
against slightest of slights, the smallest of mess.
Thesod could not scrounge a way out of this.
These nomaddy faces were angered with bliss.
With sharp swords outstretched they surrounded Thesod
and dar mofty friends, a round ringfull of mob.
They'd pay for that camel they'd eaten so snide.
They'd pay them quite dearly. They'd pay with their hides.

Thesod said, "Listen . . . about what we ate.
If you knew our camel you would not feel hate.
Our camel was nastful, a villainous yak,
whose only good point was the hump on his back.
He wouldn't bear burdens or help out at all
in our journey through desert. He had lots of gall.
He'd kick at our feets and then spit on our backs,
and he'd eat all our swill right from out of our packs.

I know for a fact he weren't camel entire,
with camel for mother, but scrub mule for sire.

And his two parents weren't pure breds the least,
with mother part jackass and part wildebeest.
His father was scrub mule, and his other half
was humpty-backed burro and knob-head Giraffe.
And so I maintain it weren't wrongful repast.
Our camel (in more ways than one) . . . was an ass."

Vim, Zed, and Gom chimed in quick at this time,
"Thesod is right. It would be a crime
to kill us outright when we weren't ruled-out wrong!
This camel was not who you'd want to know long,
but we knew him well. Too well, as a fact.
The few things he did to be nice were an act."

Zed added in, "I once saw him write home
to his mother who lives in a pen all alone.
He wrote her, 'Dear Mother, I know you need food,
and once I get paid, pray don't think me rude,
but don't think that you'll see a bit of this dough.
I won't give you any, as you full well know.'

To grandmother camel he wrote up this phrase,
'You're senile, old cow. That you live I'm amazed.'"
Gom said, "Don't punish at all for this deed.
We merely rid Orn of foul bane in our need!"

Hatter considered the tales of this gang,
thinking quite smart that they too quickly sang
of the faults of a camel that he'd never met.
He couldn't be sure but he would make a bet
that this story was made up of lying tall tales.
They'd be disappointed when stories all failed.
Hatter said, "How do we know this is true?
You slander a camel whose life is long through.
I've never seen camels pen letters to ken,
especially letters foul-writ with cross pen.
I'll give you one minute to retell your lies
and turn them to truths, or I'll make you all die."

Said Thesod to mofts, "We tried all our best,
but seems that right now we all go to our rest.
Remember me well when we meet down below,
in dark realm of Tartarsauce[126] and God Playdough[127].

Bane Camel

The nomads shrieked loudly and unsheathed their blades
to kill this brave crew that now trembled afraid.
But just as their swords all whizzed toward these clowns,
the sand opened up and it swallowed them down.

Thesod and mofts fell down into the sand,
escaping their fate at the hands of that band.
But what was the price? Would they die down below?
No one knew whither which way they did go.
They fell and they fell and they fell and they fell
down shafts of gray rock like an unfinite well.
Just when they thought that their lives would sure end,
they started to slow and they bounced 'round a bend.

Part XIII. The Saving Dwarvies

Far down below from the nast sandy world
Thesod's and dar mofts' fair brains were a-whirled
from their quickish descent and their landing quite rough.
They looked all around and they rubbed their sore duffs.
They stood in a grotto made up of white stone,
frightened and cold, but they were not alone.
On each every side they saw eyes peeping out
from tiny holes carved in the walls all about.
Asudden doors opened and dwarvies[128] stomped in
laughing quite gladly and crating a din.
They nice-smiled at Thesod and green noseful crew
while pulling at whiskers and viewing the view.

Graymaned Andvarri[129], the stout Dwarvie chief,
offered his hand. Dar mofts laughed with relief.
Dwarfchief said, "Welcome to Karlsgood[130], good man.
We'll treat you much better than nomadly band.

Freya[131] our Goddess saw much in her thoughts
and told us to help you if you did get caught

by the nomadly rowdies in desert up high.
We opened a hole, and we hoped you'd drop by.

Let me acquaint you with dwarves here and all.
Here on my left side are Thor Lowerdahll,
Ziggurny (the Weaver), and Urda (girl-Skald),
Mumble the Wise, and Egg-Dweezle the Bald,
Ymil the Giant[132], and there in the door,
Xerkies the Sorceress[133], felled from Azgourd[134].

Xerkies approached them with peach-pitting smile
and said to Andvarri, "I'll take them awhile.
You are too busy with leaderly chores,
so I'll take them each to their cozy rooms' doors."

Andvarri was grateful for Xerkies attempt
to take care of strangers, quite tired and unkempt.
He left them to the Spellflinger's good care
and went to his work in this underground lair.

Xerkies did lead them through labyrinthine ways,
here going left and, there, down steps stonegrey,
then going right, left, and straight for a time.

The Saving Dwarvies

Of all other dwarvies they saw not a sign.
Lastly they reached a huge, thick wooden door
and entered right in across wide blue-slabbed floor.

In the long trip through this Gnostrian maze[135]
tired Thesod had lost all the rest while adaze.
He rushed all about in long, cold empty halls,
scanning all doorways, examining walls.
Thesod turned left down a darkly lit pass
that buzzied with insects which bit and harrassed.
Brave Thesod stumbled and fell and did shout,
which let a large bug fly right into his mouth.
[His view of the insect was not very clear,
so Thesod did not know the bug was no mere
low insect without any powers at all.
This bug, on its back had a spell written small
saying, "No mortal's spell can now harm you the least
today, if upon this large bug you do feast."]
Thesod hard-swallowed and grimaced his face,
and then walked away with a rapidfull pace.

Xerkies had made her intentions quite clear
to dar mofts (who laughed in the corner with fear).

Her new pig collection was getting real low,
and, lucky enough, some replacements did show.
Xerkies turned dar mofts to laughing green swine
who snooted and snuffled and had a swill time.

Thesod walked in and he glared at the witch,
daring her now for her pigspells to pitch.
She chanted and sputtered, but Thesod did not
turn boarish or swinish by even a jot.
Gaping at Thesod, mad Xerkies drew back
as Thesod drew sword and then threatened attack.
"Turn all my crew back to dar mofts!" he yelled.
"Turn them all back or you've spelled your last spell!"

Laughing Green Swine

Part XIV. The prophet sees prophecies

Xerkies said sadly, "Please do not slay me,
for I just now unspelled and made your crew free
of their green swinish fates in these caverns so low!
Please, do not slay me! By thirdsight[136] I'll show
a route you should take so your journey go well.
I strongly suggest that you all go to hell!!!
In foul Tartarsauce a great wiser you'll heed,
awesome Tieclippias[137], wiser of Queebs.
Through doorway behind you you'll enter foul place,
if you have the innards for Playdough to face."

Just then Andvarri approached from the rear.
He'd reckoned that Xerkies had acted bit queer.
He said, "Do not blame her, a sickness she's got.
Swine Flu's[138] made the rounds. It's a bad dose she's caught.
Goodly Andvarri appologized well
and begged them to stay there and not visit hell.

"Hatees is neighbor to us here below.
He's not a bad guy, but I'd like you to know
that most of his guests don't enjoy their long stay.

They yell and they bellow. For salvation they pray."
Thesod replied with a gleam in his eye,
"Thank you, good dwarvie, but driven am I."

Thesod and dar mofts did open foul port
to enter a realm of real icky, nast sort.
Waiting a-door was a beastful, big dog
with three big-jawed heads and a bark like a frog.
Doggie, named Autobus[139], forced them to sign
visitor's passes. Good until nine.

Playdough mistrusted these nine bravish souls
but signed all their passes, accepted the toll.
He bade them to go (looking fearsomely Godded),
to visitors' cavern, well worn and much trod.
[Santaklos, pasty-faced God of the Dead,
was off on vacation, perhaps at Club Dread[140].
This was quite lucky for Thesod and men,
for Santaklos didn't much like Freeny then
and was the whole cause for their mission so dire.
They practically walked from the pan to the fire.]

Zed got out karmel[141] to call out the shades
and sloshed it in troughs that were there, ready-made.
Thesod watched grimly with band of dar mofts
as the dead took a break to get sweets from the trough.
He was much en-horrored by sight of the dead,
shambling and moaning and looking unfed.
Everyone knew of the deads' sweetened tooths[142],
and dead shoved each other and proved out this truth
as they tried to be first to the nectar a-trough.
They pushed all away, even Thesod and mofts.

Thesod drew sword to hold vile shades at bay
while searching for Queeb-wiser. Needle in hay.
He looked at his eight-by-ten glossy in hand,
examining features of this dead wise man,
comparing them to the dead rabble all round.
The awesome Queeb-wiser was not to be found.
Thesod called out to the sweet-slurping shades
asking if anyone knew where had strayed
the wiser from Queebs with the red, bulgy nose.
Deep in the thronging a shrill voice arose,
"He's in the bathroom, O'bringer of sweets.
He'll be here shortly, so just take a seat."

When awesome Ticlippias came to the band

he had quite good prophecies ready to hand.

He told them the Dwarvies would build them a kree

with which they should sail south, northeast in wide sea.

They'd need to plug ears when they passed Tocsin Isle[143]

where Sirens[144] exert all their decibelled wiles.

Through Straits of Nujursey[145] they'd dare monsters nast,

Skyler and Cherrypits[146], vicious and vast.

In a short time they would reach Kroft's far shores,

finding salvation (perhaps less or more).

The Underwhere

Part XV. Sailing the Golden Behind

Thesod and dar mofts to Karlsgood returned
bearing with them the good foresights they'd learned.
As wise Queeb-man said, the fine dwarvies were glad
to build a lead kree from lead surplus they had.
So for three weeks dwarvies slaved at this job,
using fine skills learned from Festus, the God[147].
They built a great kree on the near shores of Farr,
with sleek hull of lead and wide tine-sails a-spar,
and named her quite fondly "The Golden Behind."
(They ran out of lead and used gold they did mine.)
Thesod and dar mofts full-loaded their kree
and drifted out slowly to turn to the sea.
Dwarvies all cheered the fine captain and crew
and "welcomed" the "thank-yous" now yelled out anew.

Thesod and dar mofts sailed south by northeast
fearing no man, woman, child, or nast beast
as they kept to their journey to Kroft far afield.
They knew fairly well what the future would yield.
The twenty-first day brought them nigh Tocsin Isle,
so they sped their Behind and then readied awhile.

Thesod and dar mofts squished muck in their ears
to stymie the noises afar they did hear.
As they sailed closer, all dimmed through the muck,
they heard blasts, and bugles, and loud fire trucks,
battle cries, whistles, and bells ringing grand.
The noise was enough to en-deafen all hands.

Thesod was tempted to hear these fine sounds
and unmucked his ears while the dar mofts did bound
his arms to the mast with some lashings from tines.
After five minutes he did not feel fine.
He bellowed to dar mofts for bondings to cut,
but they could not hear him and loud-answered, "What?"
After much time of a-miming while bound,
Thesod did manage to bring mofts around
to lessen his ties and release him anew.
(By this time Tocsin Isle faded from view.)
Dar mofts asked captain which way they should sail.
Thesod said, "What?" for his hearing did fail.
Ten days more at sea saw fierce Cape Bortlevin,
its skraggy, red cliffs and the reefings of sin[148].
Heeding advice which the Queeb-wiser gave,
they stayed clear of cliffies and Skyler's death-cave.

They knew Skyler had many sticky, long arms.
Sail too far west and they'd all buy the farm[149].
However, they couldn't go too far to east,
for Cherrypits waited, a whirlpooling beast,
with hundreds of flippers awork splashing wild
like big, angry flatdemons[150], freaked and enriled.

Skyler roared loudly, his tantallers[151] flailed,
as all his attempts to eat moftmeat did fail.
Cherrypits spun, making deadly whirlspines
and tried hard to paddle the Golden Behind.
Her seaweedy face grimaced up from the sea,
but Thesod and dar mofts were safe in their kree.
The Golden Behind left behind the foul strait
and all of the beasties there nastly await.

Westwinds blew northly in East-Westly Sea[152]
as kree sailed on slowly to Kroft proud and free.
After ten days the crew saw land come near,
and what they did see as they more closely peered,
were finely, fine castles with spires high above,
and temples of Great Afrodainty of Love.

They cringed down below as loud flapping they heard.
Was this flapping Godly, or was it a bird?
They hoped they would not hear Quickslivver this time,
flapping in fastly with message divine
of more Godly torments against to defend
now that they came at their long journey's end.
They realized the flapper was Love-bird divine[153].
The Goddess of Love had sent them a good sign.

Between Skyler & Cherrypits

Part XVI. To fray or not to fray

Kroft was majestic, a city much grand,
the biggest and bestest in all of the land.
The streets were twist-twisty and wended for miles,
and buildings were sky-ticklers, glossed with gold tiles.
Throngs in the streets bought and sold Kroft's fine wares
at top-notchest market, the Kroft Bizarre Fair[154].

Thesod and crew were in awe at the sights
of so many strange folks, and buildings' great heights,
and riches and splendors and foods[155] of all sort.
They saw all these things just one mile from Kroft port.
Before them they saw that it got much more grand,
with buildings thrice taller and decor unbland.

They pressed through the great, teeming throngs in the streets.
They had their fate and a Goddess to meet,
but that did not keep them from sampling some wares
and eating prime foods at this wondrous Kroft Fair.

An old, baldy beggar did follow them 'round
the streets of the market, with breath-wheezy sounds.

"Have ye extra smoolies[156] for old man like me
who once fought in battles afar over sea
'gainst beasties and warriors and Death's pasty hand.
Have ye extra smoolies for such of a man?"

"O' Great Goddess Hairless," laughed Thesod. "Fine bum!"
Your blue, Goddish aura sticks out like sore thumbs!"
At that baldy beggar reformed with a whiff
to Blue Goddess Hairless, a little bit miffed
that Thesod so easily sniffed her pretense.
Seems that his mission had given him sense.

"I've come here to offer my Godful advice
to you, my brave Thesod, for I am so nice.
Now that you've come to your brave journey's close,
there are two pathways from which you can chose.
My personal pick is the dungeonly way
past real nast guard-beasties for frenze-bloody fray,

and thence through the pits of nast slowsand[157] below.
Of sneaking approach Afrodainty won't know.
Then you can steal the Love-Treasure[158], so keen,
to barter with Goddess to save your fair Freen."

This said Blue Hairless, blood-gleam in her eyes,
hoping for braveness and dangerous vies.

Thesod said softly, "I don't like that one.
What is the other way that could be done?"
Hairless then slighted his ancestors loud
and quick asked of him, "Be you not at all proud?
You turn down my offers for danger and death
with timid protestings and wimpy lungs' breath.
The easiest way you can save frightened Freen
is to knock on the door and but ask to be seen
by Great Afrodainty. She'll certain lend hand
to man (or a wimp) with such love for his land."
With blueblinding flash Goddess Hairless did leave
without a good-bye and quite Goddessly peeved.

"Well, gentlemofts," Thesod said with loud-smile,
lastly we've reached the Love-Temple turnstiles[159].
Now comes the time to seek Goddessly aid.
This I must do by myself, I'm afraid.
Wait for me here outside Love Dance Hall doors,
and I will return before you can get bored."

Thesod bought tickets to enter fine place
(TEN PFENNS[160] A DANCE each did say on its face).
Inside the Hall the Love-priestesses sat,
short, young, old, dark, fair-skinned, tall, thin, or fat,
waiting for some brave men willing to chance
paying 10 pfenns for a short, waltzie dance.
These brave men lost all their braveness when faced
with dancing and basking in Great Love-Goddess grace,
so they gazed from afar by the bandstandly stage
at priestesses with a love-sheepishly gaze.
Thesod quick-crossed the uncrowded dance floor
to timidly knock-knock on Goddessly door.

Afrodainty, Goddess of Love

Part XVII. Alot for naught, but fair is Fare

Answering door in maewestian grace
Pink Afrodainty, all dressed in white lace,
invited bold Thesod inside to confer
about what he needed to request from her.
She sashayed around winking blue-lidded eyes
and, smoking from long-filtered cigs, giant-sized,
she asked him a question from side of her lips,
"What took you so long, honey? Beast get your ship?"

Thesod did tell her of all his ordeals,
sea beasties, stormings, oft eating no meals,
nomadly desert and Hatees below,
Hotel Calypso and goo-berry dough.
Mostly he told her of Syrinx of Fare
and love that he had new-discovered while there.
All of these things he had done for fair Freen,
always remembering times there were lean.

Great Afrodainty rolled blue-lidded eyes,
releasing aloud sympathetical sighs.
"I'm sorry, your journey was all for the vain
for Gods became bored with inflicting of pain

on fine Freeny two weeks after you had been gone.
The Gods they did use you as playthingly pawn.
Since your request to save Freeny is void,
and you seem frabjously, greatly annoyed,
perhaps I could grant you some other request,
like make you immortal[161] and give you some rest
as stand-full of reeds, or a pillar of sand,
star constellation, or Jub-tree quite grand.
As any of these you could live evermore,
never forgotten in Freenian lore."

Thesod, astounded by news of his land
and useless, long journey by him and his band,
could only decline her fine offers outright.
Eleven good months were now quite out of sight!!!
"Thank-you, good Goddess, for your kindly words.
Perhaps you could send me directly homewards
with kree and my crew and without trip unshort
by placing us safely a-kree in home port.
Goddess said, "Maybe when not in a bind
you'll want to come up and see me sometime."
With "whoofing" of hands she sent Thesod right home,
safely a-sound and thus ending his roams.

The Featherless Dove

Thesod and mofties, now back in fair Freen
were happy to see what they always had seen.
Nothing was new, everything in its place.
They knew a good name for each Freenian face.
Nobody asked where they'd been for such time
but asked, "Were you gone?" or worse, "Lend me a dime?"
Thesod was happy, just freed from Gods' test,
and only was wanting his castle and rest,
but what he did find when he reached his nice home
was condo-conversion and spray-painted stone.
Eleven months short on his taxes so great,
they'd re-possessed castle and sold his estate.

A featherless dove flew in north by southwest
flapping a-fastly with featherless crest,
bringing from Love Goddess message divine.
It said, "Thesod, honey, your Syrinx is fine
and wishes you back by her side once again.
Your fate is in Fare, so go seaward with men."
"Looks like we're sealubbers!" Thesod laughed hale.
"What are we waiting for, let's be asail!
Vim, Zed, Gom, Aldo, Jod, what do you say?
How 'bout you, Zeppo, and you Bob and Ray?

Will you all follow me back to fair Fare,
daring nast beasties to get us back there?"
All of the dar mofts said "Yes!" with a yelp,
"You're good for a laugh, and you need mofty help!"
So Thesod with dar mofts set sail, not a care,
to love-lovely Syrinx awaiting in Fare.

The End

Returning to Fare

Endnotes

1 The first insult of the Gods occurred in 12 YOTG. King Telly of Grommet-upon-Nilpeg (due to a very bad speech impediment) couldn't say the word "god" without inciting howls of laughter from his people. Naturally, this angered the Gods, and they turned the King into a fruit bat.

2 Ornians have an unusual time-keeping system. The hour of When is about a quarter to Now or half past Ever, whichever comes first and depending upon what time it is.

3 High God of all Gods. He was the son of Joey-boy, the God of the Sun, and Gooey, the Earthgoddess.

4 Green, pointy-headed, large-nosed, self-imposed slaves. The unknown true intellectuals of Orn

5 Santaklos, son of Playdough and Afrodainty.

6 The realm of the gods, believed to be at the very top of the not-so-tall Olmpoo Hill

7 Loud, fast, and silent beasties used by the gods to punish mortals

8 Giant killer sloths

9 Enormous murderous, yet smiley, clones

10 A popular style of dwelling built in the ancient Threedor style

11 The town leadsmithie and well known "allegator" wrestler. He settled legal disputes by wrestling lawyers in the high courts.

12 The largest of all the godly beasts, with feet half the size of its own body. Ancient Ornian saying: "Beware the Grat with dancing feet."

13 The largest city on Orn and the home of the holy Dance Halls of the Goddess of Love.

14 An Ornian sailing vessel, usually made out of the most abundant metal available . . . lead.

15 The Goddess of Love and creator of humankind (using a little bit of clay, a sense of humor, and a couple of opposable thumbs).

16 The God of Geeks (also known as the God of Pencil-necked Geeks).

17 The Goddess of Idiot Savants.

18 Northern, smelly goatlands of Freeny.

19 Tiny northwestern province of Freeny, only 20 miles square and 3 feet deep, that was famous for it's Dude ranches and banana slugs.

20 Seventy-one and a half meters, give or take seventy-one and a half meters.

21 All Ornian gods are color-coded for easy identification.

22 A unit of time somewhere between a minute and a decade.

23 Similar to the earth term "nasty" but much, much worse.

24 Having the characteristics of bulliciosity.

25 A very small, horrible-smelling nut which grows in abundance on Malodor trees.

26 Literally translated as "Town of unsightly growths on the river of deformed fish". Despite the name it is a well reputed vacation spot.

27 Orn is the only place in the universe where two rongs make a reit, and there are 2.4 reits in a henway. What's a henway? About 2 pounds.

28 Tin is an abundant element on Orn used much in sail-weaving, rope-making, and dental floss.

29 Whoo-eeeeee . . . wucka, wucka, vooooooooooooo . . . whoo-eeeeeeeeeeeeeeeeeeeeeee!
30 Feline infestation of the slime-fields of Balsa.
31 Overpopulation of Dore by rapidly-breeding fuzzy plastic products endangered the lives of the Dorians.
32 Herds of wimps blocked the streets and jeered at pedestrians, only to run frantically when mildly threatened. Innocent people were in danger from wimp stampedes.
33 Thin, gazelle-like animals which normally grazed the surrounding grasslands of Pride suddenly began grazing the thatched roofs in town when the ground became too hot for their delicate hooves.
34 Ancient Ornian spelling for tin. (Also *tinne*, *tinnnnne*, and *ye olde tine*).
35 An unusual dar moft ceremony involving the harvest of belly-button lint.
36 This dar moft who lived in Orn's earliest recored history (around 184 YOTG), is now recognized as one of the greatest Philosophers who ever lived. He once successfully determined the origin of the universe using a rubber chicken and a bag of rice.
37 Mathematical analysis of irregularities on a plain surface with absolutely no irregularities.
38 Founder of the Flat-Orn society.
39 Leaping while spinning.
40 Walking on tiptoes while in a low crouch.
41 Traditional asking of favors in a high-pitched nasal voice.
42 Freenian sailor's term for rope walkways around the sails and spars (named after the funny pigeon-toed walk used by sailors).
43 A special lead clay used for patching holes in the ship's hull (or as a sandwich spread).
44 Excruciatingly smallest.
45 It is an amazing phenomenon (well known by Ornian historians) that dar mofts become incredibly stupid and clumsy when attempting to work, yet are as graceful and clever as can be when endeavoring to avoid work (or to prove a point in a philosophical debate).
46 A low-pitched whistling noise made through the large noses of dar mofts.
47 Rather slothful avian alcoholics which ten to flock around local distilleries.
48 Young dar moft games are identical to adult dar moft games except that they are usually played by young dar mofts (but not necessarily).
49 It is unlikely that Homer is actually suggesting that the dar mofts ever worked. Historians agree that this is probably poetic license. (If poetry like this deserves a license).
50 A geographical anomaly in which storms drive large rocks leap up from the sea floor and out of the water.
51 Knobs and levers had been invented, even in this Age of Pre-Automation. However, nobody found a use for them until almost 400 years later.
52 A hard, rubber captain replica used to steady the ship's wheel.
53 As in the "late" Thesod of Freeny.
54 Passageway between the Twin Cliffs of Insanity in the Psykotic Sea.
55 Exactly like regular mime except very loud.
56 A seven-headed, seven-tailed sea-monster well known as Geeroffaneefy's "hit-beast."
57 Making the sounds "oof" and "ort".

58 Amphibious feline that lives half of its time in the water, half on land, and loves to play with wet catnip.
59 Full of brandness.
60 Thesod was trained by one of the greatest fencing wizards on Orn, Inigo the Mostly Blind.
61 A very heavy weight.
62 Perhaps induced by the blow to its heads.
63 AAAHIEOOOOARGH!
64 Hindquarters, in this case including seven butts.
65 A magic elixer created and mass-produced by Sagena, the Goddess of Occasionally Useful Things.
66 Men and women from the Guild of Prophets For Profit.
67 Few people sailed in these times because of the horrible beasties, uncharted waters, and the fear of missing their favorite puppet shows.
68 A particular hour of the day which occurs only twice a year.
69 The sound one makes on Orn when drinking in polite company.
70 Feathers from the rare feathered dolphins of Grishamur.
71 Mythical hotel on the Island of Cretin.
72 The nasal croonings of Cretins.
73 Mofts of the female persuasion.
74 Dar moftian eyeballs.
75 Exotic gourmet cottonfat, served with large chunks of frozen butter.
76 Spicey meat of deliberately unknown origin.
77 Large slabs of cake dipped in bird-lard and sugar.
78 Fake animal hide, obtained from fake animals.
79 Squid raised in the sunken poppy fields of Altsanti.
80 Also known as "that ugly, white goddess with the nasty disposition."
81 Brain stealing was common on Orn, with some thieves becoming so adept that their victims did not notice for several days, if ever.
82 Presumeably a reference to some part of the hag anatomy.
83 White was considered by Ornians to be the color of evil.
84 Fuzzy-pelted deciduous form of conifer.
85 Giant, silk-producing, carnivorous caterpillars.
86 Young and ripened to a nice, sickly green.
87 Furiously rapid, usually while whistling nervously.
88 Eelba had the power to turn men to goo-berry dough, women to hags, and children into corn muffins.
89 An ancient (and very popular) Ornian legend foretold that an insignificant-looking, slimey rock would someday be discovered, and it would make its bearer the richest and most powerful being in the 11 universes.
90 The smallest coin in the poor country of Speck. This coin was worth less than the cardboard from which it was made.
91 Also known as the "Underwhere", realm of the Gods Playdough and Santaklos.
92 Moft-Latin for "We're in big trouble! Dar mofts we'd best walk. This thing is nothing but a large, dirty rock."

93 Eelba's secret desire was to be an opera diva.
94 String woven from the hair of the Great Hairy Clam.
95 Large, finned watersloths often found in the deep sea hanging for dear life onto floating debris, since they are only able to swim for a mile at a time.
96 Black and white, limbed sea-mammals with a talent for bad mime. Often whole schools of these fish drown while "walking down stairs."
97 Large-nostrilled, barnacle-feeding fish which latch onto the hulls of ships with their noses while trying to inhale barnacles.
98 Fanged, rock-eating fish which have 4-inch jaws, 2-inch fangs, and one-inch bodies.
99 All experienced sea captains would look for the elusive constellation of the Furtive Wombat in order to orient to the east.
100 When an Ornian is proud, his chest smells of garlic.
101 Calmly faded away with almost mindless abandon.
102 The Messenger of the Gods, also known as Burmese or Flash.
103 Referring to Fare's rare Crabbicus Landicus Inediblus.
104 Indoor plumbing was unknown on Orn at this time, so nobles used aqueducts (or else just plain ducks) to transport water to outdoor bathing facilities.
105 A small but prosperous kingdom on a small continent composed of Fare, Farr, and the enormous Farihott desert.
106 Daughter of King Gummo and Queen Betty of Fare, and sister to Nauseous.
107 Dar mofts rarely take the direct approach to a problem but try to solve it in the most effectively silly way that they can.
108 Cacticus Eatmeaticus.
109 If you can imagine the most absolutely disgusting smell in the world, multiply it by one gazillion and you get a dreadnastful smell.
110 Mountain dwelling folk who can be found on almost any high mountain in the twelve universes.
111 The only country besides Fare on the continent of Farrenheit, on the opposite side of the Farihott Desert.
112 Nonhorse was believed to be an elder god of Orn, predating Moose and the rest of the gods in Olmpoo. However, he was apparently a weak and senile god, requiring Moose to enforce his godly laws.
113 Reason for exemption or for free coupons.
114 AIEE! AIEE! ACOOPEE!
115 Extinct giant, woolly Greatpig.
116 A vessel for the words of the Gods.
117 Giant sand-breathing tadpoles which are an early form of the King Sandtoad.
118 Red, porous, foamrock.
119 Colonies of sandfungus deep in the sand which served as sand-guppy food.
120 Moftian nose-flute.
121 Plural form of spouse.
122 The ancient desert empire of Nonhorse.
123 Nonhorse was the most prolific writer of all the gods, however, he often wrote the same book 10 or 12 times before he got it right.
124 The hour between Later and Early, or half-past Nowandthen.

125 Literally translated as "I'm one happy nomad!" and "Life is good again!"
126 The Underwhere realm of the dead.
127 Also known as Hatees, the God of the Underwhere, and wearer of snappy hats.
128 A breed of short, stout mining folk, famed for their metal-working and love of Parcheesi.
129 The son of the famous battle-dwarvie, Loko, who was directly descended from Odeus, the North God of Gods.
130 The deepest caverns known in the 12 universes, they are believed to be endless only because they actually are endless.
131 Queen of Dwarvies during the Dwarvian Renaissance.
132 He was descended from heartier dwarvie stock, towering over his comrades by a full 3 inches.
133 She was once the Goddess of Dwarvies, however, she became mortal when she fell in love with an adventuring mortal dwarvie (who later became immortal for heroic deeds, leaving her behind).
134 Sky realm of the North Gods.
135 Reference to King Minabird's infamous labyrinth on the island of Gnostril.
136 Any sorceress worth her weight in lead has a third eye behind her left ear which provides 20/20 hindsight and a slightly myopic view of the future.
137 He was once a blind wise man from Queebs who advised the Queebians in the Sturgeon War of 824 YOTG. He was also a well-known jazz pianist and inventor of artificial nose hair.
138 A type of influenza which causes an obsession for pork.
139 Guardian dog of the Underwhere, able to fetch three sticks at a time and keep out an infinite number of illegal visitors.
140 Anybody who was anybody in the "dead" profession vacationed at this club.
141 Sweet, sticky syrup made by karmel bees.
142 Escapees from the Underwhere often raided the candy shops of the living.
143 Also known as Toxin Isle, this tiny island waste dump was equipped with sirens to attract passing sailors who were then forced to take a doggie-bag of toxic waste home with them. Few mortal beings can resist the lure of police sirens or fire trucks.
144 Waste-management employees dwelling on Tocsin isle.
145 The dangerous sea channels of Cape Bortlevin.
146 Cherrypits was once a beautiful maiden in love with the handsome Prince Skyler. One day, while picnicking by the sea, they ridiculed the seagod Friton because of his horrible hair style and his love for sushi. In punishment the gods turned them into fearsome and deadly monsters, forever unable to be together or get good take-out food.
147 He was the God of Anvils who tripped and fell from Olmpoo, giving himself a terrible limp. In shame and embarrassment, he remained with the mortal dwarvies of Forge City and taught them the fine art of leadsmithing.
148 Coral reefs off the Straits of Nujursey with a nasty habit of wrecking evil sailors or pirates.
149 Old Ornian saying derived from the tale of Death and farmer Henry, in which Death tricks the farmer into purchasing his own death which has been cleverly disguised as a farm.
150 Vicious, giant sea-tapeworms.

151 Long, sticky arms.

152 Sea in the southern, north-central hemisphere of Orn.

153 The featherless dove.

154 The 6-month, twice annual, market fair of Kroft which often attracted strange beings and goods from other planets and universes, making for one of the most unusual occurrences on Orn.

155 The Kroft Bizarre Fair was famous for its street-muffins, snail-puffs, and insect pies. Ornian saying: "You haven't been in Kroft if you haven't eaten something strange."

156 Ornian term for a coin roughly equivalent to an Earthly American dollar.

157 Bottomless pits of sucking sand which are full of sand sharks and other foul beasts.

158 Most of the world's Love was kept safe in Afrodainty's vault. If there was too much love in the world, life would be sickeningly sweet and no one would take it seriously, so Afrodainty only rewarded deserving souls with love.

159 The Love-Temple was a very popular place, so it was created with large crowds in mind. There were 50 turnstiles and 138 ticket booths serving 12 enormous Dance Halls.

160 Ten pfenns = 110 smoolies, give or take 100 smoolies.

161 The highest compliment that a god could bestow upon a mortal was turn the mortal into a rock or some other such long-lasting thing, since they considered mortality to be a disgusting habit.